D1108921

Get the most
out of this book.

Look at the illustrations first, then read the black text.
The purple text sprinkled throughout provides added information for your growing learner (or for you!).

What's around you?
Take the opportunity to relate what's in the book to real life. Here are some ideas:
- When reading about neurons, point to your little one's head and tell them they are in there.
- Point to flowers and ask about size differences (at home and in the book).
- Count the flowers and inquire about colors (at home and in the book).
- Ask how different machines make life easier and fun (in and outside the home).
- Point out smart machines that can learn (in and outside the home).

Build on after story time
Take everyday moments to observe and talk about science and technology. Look for opportunities to highlight examples in the book. For instance, ask where the 'brain' for machines you encounter are (either at home or when you're out and about). Neuro shows us his brain can be in his head or stomach. These are occasions to turn everyday experiences into fun, informal learning opportunities!

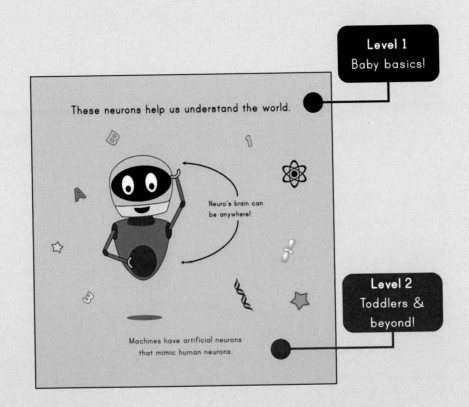

These neurons help us understand the world.

Neuro's brain can be anywhere!

Machines have artificial neurons that mimic human neurons.

Level 1
Baby basics!

Level 2
Toddlers & beyond!

Neuro
the robot

Jaya

To Yuri,
thank you for your guidance and support
in all my creative endeavors these past few years.

No part of this book is to be duplicated or commercialized without explicit permission from the publisher.

Registered trademark & copyright © 2020 by GenBeam, LLC.
Book, cover and internal design by GenBeam, LLC.
Cover and internal illustrations © 2020 by GenBeam, LLC.
Published in the United States by GenBeam, LLC.
All rights reserved.

Visit us on the Web!
www.tinkertoddlers.com

Contact us!
tinkertoddlerbooks@gmail.com

Tinker Toddlers supports early STEM learning. STEM is an acronym for science, technology, engineering, and mathematics. We provide simple explanations about emerging STEM concepts to the littlest learners to help facilitate the absorption of complex details later in life.

Introducing STEM early has shown to improve aptitude in math, reading, writing and exploratory learning in a wide spectrum of topics.

Neural Networks!

for KiDS

Dr. Dhoot

Do you like flowers?

Jaya likes flowers, a lot!

She's learning about different sizes.

BIG

small

What is your
favorite flower?

Machines can learn, too!

Neuro can learn to find different flower sizes.

A vacuum can learn to clean.

A smart speaker can learn to play music you like.

A car can learn to drive itself.

A drone can learn to find forest fires.

Let's see *how* Jaya and Neuro learn!

Learning units in the brain are called **neurons**.

Jaya's brain is in her head, just like yours!

These neurons help us understand the world.

Neuro's brain can be anywhere!

Machines have artificial neurons
that mimic human neurons.

This is a neuron in Jaya's brain.

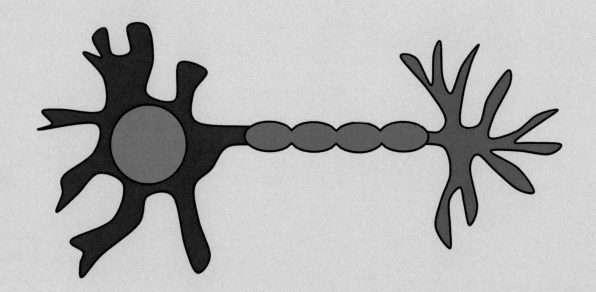

Neurons in humans have **dendrites**,
a cell body, an axon and axon terminals.

These are neurons in Neuro's brain.

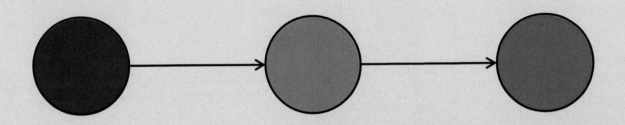

Neurons in machines, called nodes, have **input**,
hidden, and **output** layers.

In Jaya's neuron...

...information comes in...

...is analyzed...

Flower Size
Flower Color

...passed on...

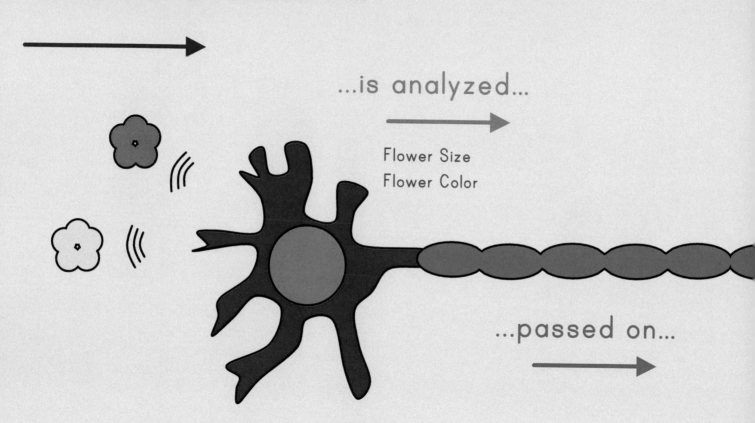

Information is fed to the brain from
your eyes, nose, ears, mouth, and skin.

... and results flow out!

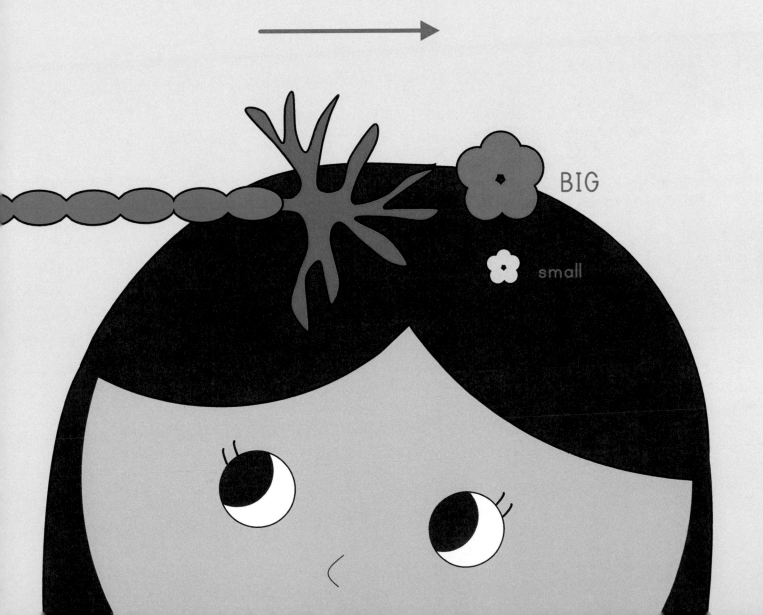

BIG

small

In Neuro's neurons...

...information comes in...

... is analyzed...

Flower Size
Flower Color

Information is fed or
presented to the machine.

... and results flow out also!

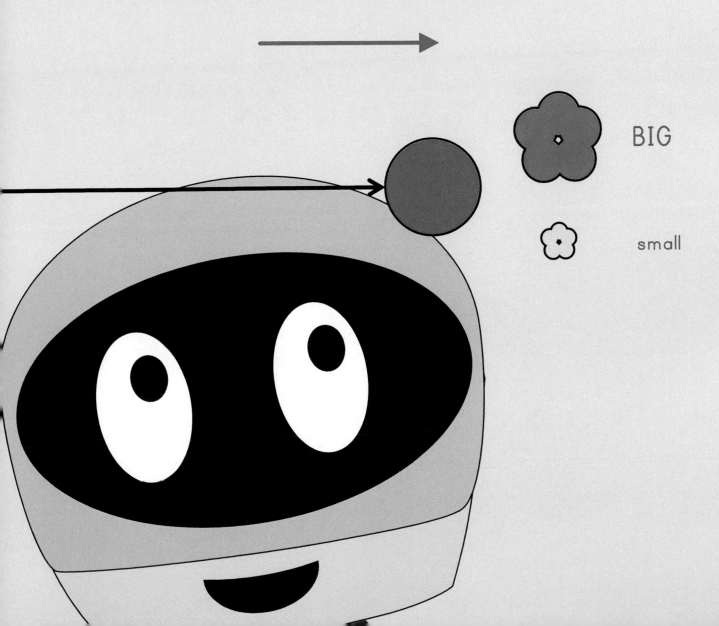

BIG

small

Jaya's neurons talk to each other.

Information in   analyze   results →   Information in   analyze   results →

A web of neurons form Jaya's neural network!

(we have ~100 billion neurons)

Neuro's neurons talk to each other also!

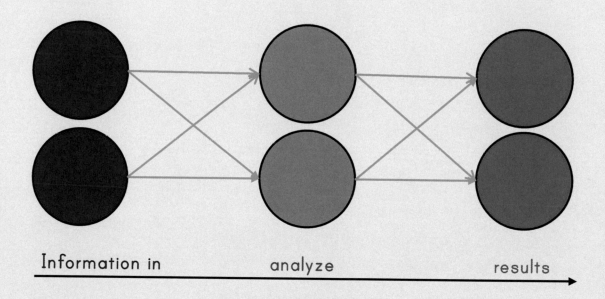

Information in   analyze   results

Training helps hidden neurons
learn to make decisions.

A web of machine neurons form
Neuro's neural network!

The more Jaya learns,

How many flowers
are in Jaya's basket?

the more her **neural network**
knows and grows!

The more Neuro learns,

How many flowers are
in Neuro's basket?

the more his neural network
knows and grows!

Now Neuro knows about
BIG and small flowers...

...just like us, and more!

How many BIG and small flowers can you count?

Neural networks help machines learn so they can solve hard problems faster!

Neuro can now identify more flowers.

Neuro uses his neural network to learn new things.

Neuro can give us answers fast!

When machines help us...

...we have more time for play!

How many
flowers did Jaya give
to her mom?

What do you want to teach Neuro?

Glossary

Axon: the part of a neuron that takes signals away from the cell body.

Axon terminal: the end of a neuron that sends information.

Cell body: the neuron's life-support center.

Dendrite: the part of the neuron that receives information.

Hidden Layer: in artificial neural networks, the layer in between the input and output layer where all the analysis and calculations are done.

Input Layer: in artificial neural networks, where information gets put into the neural network.

Neural Network: a web of cells that work together to produce a desired result. Each cell is responsible for passing along information. Human neural networks inspired the creation of artificial neural networks, which help computers learn.

Neuron: a special cell that carry information through your nervous system and help you learn.

Output Layer: in artificial neural networks, the last layer of a neural network that produces given outputs.

Questions for your budding learner

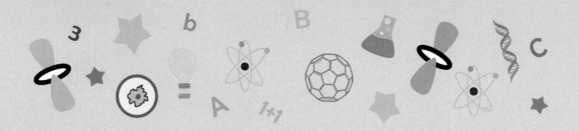

Machines help us to get work done.
What would you want to teach a machine?

Machines are everywhere.
What machines do you have at home?

The robot in this book is a machine. Its name is Neuro.
If you had a robot, what would it look like?

Draw it out on the next page and share it on Amazon by posting a review!

My Robot_____

Dear Reader,

I hope that you enjoyed reading about how machines learn.

Science and technology are evolving rapidly and it can be hard to keep up.
I hope you and your little learners enjoy learning the very basics and
continue to build on them.

If you liked this story and want to read more like it, there is a whole
series of Tinker Toddlers books on Amazon, just waiting for you.

Best,

Dr. Dhoot

www.TinkerToddlers.com
tinkertoddlerbooks@gmail.com

Tinker Toddlers' Growing Library

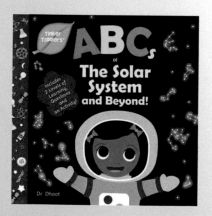

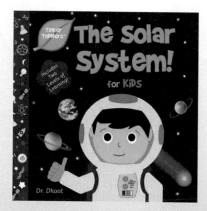

amazon.com/author/drdhoot

tinkertoddlerbooks@gmail.com

Industry experts, scientists, engineers,
parents, and kids contribute much of their time to ensure
Tinker Toddlers is successful at supporting early STEM learning.

To support our efforts, please:

1) go to order history at place of purchase
2) locate product
3) click on "write a product review"
4) tell us what your favorite part was

Made in the USA
San Bernardino, CA
27 May 2020

72384280R00022